Broken

Publications

A
Pacific Northwest
Publisher

The Silent Pond
James G. Piatt

Printed and bound in the United States of America.

First printing, 2012

ISBN-10: 0982858779
ISBN-13: 978-0-9828587-7-6

Published by Broken Publications

Broken Publications
PO Box 685
Eatonville, WA 98328

www.BrokenPublications.com

Edited by Jennifer-Crystal Johnson
www.JenniferCrystalJohnson.com

Book cover art by Wallace Piatt
www.wallaceisart.com

Table of Contents

The Silent Pond

The silent pond lies so still, its
face clear molten glass, its sides
stretching to cliffs of shale, bent
down to receive its soft coolness.

Gentle zephyrs crease its skin,
causing ripples on its ageless features.
Oh, gentle pond, how I venerate you
as you lounge in your moistened serenity.

Flowing

Sounds of water fleeing
Over smooth stones
Created by eons of years
In a mountain brook,

Nature's symphony shaped
By warm, gentle winds,
Performing an aria through
Huge, gnarled pine trees,

A ballet of Oak leaves
Swaying gently,
Green-clad pixies dancing
With tranquil delight!

These are the things
That flow in my
Mind, sitting by
A tranquil pond!

A Soul at Peace

On top of a peaceful knoll,
I sense a calming serenity
as balmy zephyrs caress me,
pulling me into stillness

Breaths of soft white cotton
hanging silently above;
green-topped mountains unite
with sighs of deep azure skies

The sun's soothing
summer-day beams
warm my hungry mind,
calm my searching heart

Softly and quietly,
my healing soul soars,
peacefully riding on the
smooth currents of time

My thoughts flow with the wind
amidst tall pines and cerulean skies,

they vibrate softly and gently,
their rhythms so peaceful:

Birch trees swaying gently
in my misty vision,
appease the thunder within,
bringing me tranquility:

Soft pine needles and tiny cones
strewn like umber-colored jewels
over faintly traveled deer paths,
cover my remaining sorrows

Slender, gnarled Oak branches
bending down to shade me,
noiselessly cause my heart
to swing lightly in gentle winds

Deep, translucent water, flowing
like colorful, splintered glass,
severing my final, sad thoughts,
refresh my sorrowful spirit:

Opposites combine wordlessly

Within all the lonely caves
inside my searching soul,
bring God's solutions to life:

Once again, that I which is really I,
Is in tune with that, which is
infinitely serene, loving, and
moreover so peaceful!

Beside a Brook

While I sit beside the brook, flowing softly
across boulders and mossy granite stone,
I dream that lazy trout are swimming there all
alone... however, dreaming doesn't make things
true, like clouds in the sky are not really pirate
ships of a ghostly hue. As I sit on the warm sand
listening to the songs of gaudy birds, as
Egrets sail gently over the ponds and frogs
croak their happy words, I view the white Birch
Trees swaying to and fro, hoping the lazy time
will continue to advance so slow, and the day
will travel extra long, like a sweet and haunting song.

The Coming of Spring

I sit by a gentle, flowing stream
Playing my ancient Indian flute,
Translucent water flows
Slowly across smooth pebbles
Of green, brown, and white, nature's
Sculptures of transparent gypsum:

I listen to the soft rustling
Of singing Sycamore leaves
In a verdant butte far away;
I marvel at a pin-tailed deer
As it leaps in sheer delight
At its unlimited freedom;
I listen to the soft cooing of
A covey of grey California quail
As the wind blows softly through
White- and gray-barked trees,
Hugging the sides of a flowing stream:

I gaze at the soft blue sky
With delicate white clouds
Moving, so lacy and frail,
The sun's gentle rays caress
My shoulders, warming them;
I squeeze the soft, smooth pebbles
Beneath my toes and watch silently
As countless speckled rainbow trout
Swim lazily down the flowing stream
To safer havens, in the pale yellow sand:

I am far away from common trials,
Stressful demands of men and life,
But within my ever-searching soul, as
I sense the world's gaunt loneliness,
Tears flow gently down my face.

Sunny Summer Days

The air, diffused with fiery arias
of youthful, vibrant joys
inspires gentle thoughts,
soft, chiming memories;
hot, precious summer days
painted with shafts of gold,
secret times.

I yield my soul to the moment,
play the child again,
romping happily in warm thoughts,
I dream of past sunny days, and
my heart blossoms.

Your Loving Presence

The lake's silver painted hue,
reflecting images from moon beams,
echoes the sadness of my thoughts
as I muse alone, I long for a song without sorrows.

I search among the thousand liquid lights
in the ebony softness above for answers;
I follow my nightmares into the shadows
beyond the safety of my soul; and,
where colored jewel feelings once gleamed
I find only dull pebbles of black sadness.

Only amid the happiness of past memories
where my heart controls my brain,
moreover, only when there is no darkness
can I find serenity, in my mind!

Images Reflected in a River

The tender murmur of translucent water
fleeing softly over ancient stones
creates a poetic aria of beautiful words,
sounds created by eons of years;
metaphors flowing in a mountain stream,
nature's calming symphony shaped
by cool, gentle currents of air
performing to a silent audience curving
through huge gnarled Sycamore and Pine trees....

A colorful ballet of wind-tossed Oak leaves
swaying so gently and serenely
like tiny green-clad pixies dancing
with a tranquil delight in themselves

Painted in the wind is the softness of her face;
the ripple of the cool breeze restores
memories and brings insight into my love,
her graying auburn hair and brown eyes
are reflected in the soft movement of the rill,
her smile echoed in the never-ending aria
her movements portrayed in the swaying
of the pixies dancing so daintily in the lea

I sense the object of my love in the sweetness
of the verdant trees and the slow movement of
the transparent stream as it meanders down the
gentle slope to the bottom of my heart;
it reflects the truth of love to my searching mind.

The Brook

Offer me your curving,
winsome voice
as you sidle
slowly
past my wandering mind,
press cool moisture
upon my body,
offer me your
buoyancy
and your ancient music,
as you chant your
melody of flowing serenity,
offer me your pleasant
breath
of a thousand suns;
Bathe me
in the coolness
of
your
essence.

Atop a Mountain

Pine needles gently fallen
Across faint deer paths
Strewn like colored jewels
Cover my sorrow and pain

Deep blue water flowing
Like colorful, splintered glass
Severing my sad thoughts
Refreshing my sorrowful spirit

The sun's soft, soothing
Beams of a summer day
Warms my hungry soul
And calms my longing heart

On top of this peaceful knoll
I find a cool serenity
As warm zephyrs caress me
Pulling me into stillness

Puffs of soft white cotton
Hanging silently above
Green mountains erupting
Into deep azure skies

Birch trees swaying so softly
In my blurry line of vision
Calms my thunderous thoughts
And brings me serenity

Slender gnarled Oak branches
Bending down to greet my sorrow
Noiselessly bring my heart
To swing lightly in gentle winds

My soul flows like the wind
Amidst tall pines and blue skies
It pours forth soothing
Rhythms, silver and silent
Opposites silently combine
Within all the lonely caves
In my searching mind

Bringing answers to life
Softly and quietly
My soul-mind soars
Up peacefully atop
Smooth currents of time

Mountain Top Experience

Umber-colored oaks with soft, fluttering leaves
Silence the pain of my darkened thoughts,
My tired and worried mind is bathed in peace:
I leave my worldly cares far below
As I listen to nature's healing rhythms.

A private abode mid pines and oaks
Soothes my search for frantic pursuits that
Lie far below these peaceful mountains,
Up here only a silent stillness is heard;
I forget to grasp happy hours below.

We rush through our daily lives
Searching for life's confusing answers.
Up here warm, soft winds, hot sun,
Smells of musty pine and oak
Cleanse anxious hearts of their pain.

Pinecones strewn like dark brown jewels
Give my eyes a contemplative serenity,
Footsteps on brown and gnarled bark,
Peaks covered with soft silver mist
Send inner vibrations to soothe my soul.

My anxious mind rests in a gentle peace,
Soft blue skies paint away my emptiness.
I pity those below, struggling with empty lives,
Up here warm and silent waves of sun
Wash my cares away, as my soul soars peacefully.

Adieu

Adieu to the clear, meandering streams,
A moist comfort to my youthful quest.
The cerulean wandering of my peaceful dreams,
A fertile place; I was welcomed as a happy guest.

My soul lives near the twisting rill, where my
Heart found solace in its vast, leafy domain.
Adieu to the falling shale that cracked so shrill,
The contentment I found there will always remain.

As I Sit Alongside a Stream

Blue wisps of smoke spiraling from an old cigar,
Melancholy music echoing from a radio
Softly streaming rhythms through my mind.
A languid pond, motionless as God's silence,
Sits serenely in front of my gaze
As a soft, warm breeze ruffles the leaves of
White birch trees, thoughts occur and
Reoccur in my wistful mind. Past dreams
Flash in and out of my fading
Memories, like the fish in the pond.
Pieces of loosened green moss
Float undisturbed in the serene pool.

Small, gaudy birds hidden high
In the limbs of tall Sycamore trees,
Sway like colorful pixies in
The gentle wind: I ponder on things
Gained and lost; upon those dreams which
Still echo across my aging mind.
The Arab spring is waning now,
Democracy still a fleeting hope,
Bodies piled high in the bitter sand,
Now an American spring is starting.
I wonder as I muse about life, what
Is going to happen to America,
In this dark era of dissent, separation, and
Chaos.

After the Storm

After the storm,
after ghostly winds
abated,
soft mountainous clouds,
scudding silently
with moisture's burden,
gratefully dropped
onerous moisture –
like a homeless man
ridding himself of
his feelings,
of hopelessness:

in the verdant leas
below,
colorful spring buds
embedded in damp soil
begin to grow.

The plentiful sun,
orange and bright,
beaming heat
from the sky,
leaves a softness,
gentle and warm,
for the coming of
a pleasant
night.

The Oak Tree's Voices

I hear the
oak tree's summer voices,
theirs is
a woody, whispering language;
Their words
fall like brown leaves upon my soul,
their
acorn verbs float in the wind,
curling around
drooping trunks,
their nouns oaken and
sturdy,
their crusty adjectives wind around
protruding knots and
twisted, gnarled limbs,
their mossy adverbs,
swift as a gale,
lift me
to heights,
far above,
my wandering
winter thoughts.
Then, in the threshold of
the icy season,
the brisk winds swiftly
denude the voices
in preparation for
winter, and
the crushing snow will
blunt the voices

until the wakening of
spring, and
then new voices of
blossoms, which will
bring emerald poems
and rhythmic songs of
praise
to my yearning
winter thoughts.

In the Meadow of Our Memories

In the meadow of our memories, new thoughts grow
Amid the roses, lilacs, pansies, and buds arow
They mark our place under azure sky
Where hawks, doves, and sparrows fly
Scarcely heard are gloomy words of woe.

We are alive, live and love, without a foe:
Holding hands with hearts aglow,
Sitting in an aged swing sans shoes and tie,
In the meadow of our memories

We sit and sway with hands in tow:
Dream new dreams swinging to and fro
Our thoughts soar high into the sky,
Creating new, happy dreams, row by row,
In the meadows of our memories.

Summer has Come to Stay

Sweet visions of warm sands have come to stay,
The ocean's tide arriving calm and still: the
Icy breath of winter no longer reflected in snow.

Frozen streams and barren trees can't dismay,
My summer heart is light and holds a thrill:
Sweet visions of warm sands have come to stay;

Cold thoughts no longer linger as winter winds decay,
The mountains no longer white with winter's chill: the
Icy breath of winter no longer reflected in snow.

Unfriendly winds once blew icy and gray,
Turning the sun dark to the iceman's will; But now
Sweet visions of warm sands have come to stay.

Unfriendly blasts of winter have gone away, no
Cold thoughts gust into the verdant hill:
The icy breath of winter no longer reflected in snow.

In months ahead, warm times will not go away,
Sunnier days will be reflected upon a rill,
Sweet visions of warm sands have come to stay, the
Icy breath of winter no longer reflected in snow.

Dreams

Near the stream where I often dream,
moreover, watch butterflies flit and fly,
far above in the deep cobalt sky,
feelings from the verdant hills do teem
into my questioning mind, so unforeseen;
and, into the inflexible earth, so hard and dry;
dark clouds scud with not a sigh, and
fish dart swiftly up the flowing stream:
my idle dreams continue to wander
to and fro, from thought to thought,
finally arriving, upon war's bloody lore.
My saddening mind has but to ponder
the dark feelings that are fraught
with images of the colossal gore.

The Peaceful Silence of My Longings

Blue-green waves explode over mossy boulders,
the turbulence of the sea tosses white foam
high into the air, and the perpetual beads of brine
upon my face enlighten my rootless senses.

The relentless current of the ocean silences
strident screams of darkness, forever fleeing
into sweltering sand as the scents of the past
roam peacefully in the crevices of my soul.

As the tide wanes, the fullness of the never-ending
hours of perpetual anticipation merge
into the briny dreams, which vanish into
the peaceful silence of my longings.

An Ocean's Sonnet

Open to all minds, hidden grandeur calls
on white-topped waves atop a mist-borne night,
the ocean roars, gnarled wood strewn a fright,
a tiny rill crawls and a swift stream falls
down jagged cliffs with spurts and palls,
these are alike in God's unequivocal might,
all water emulates the one infinitely bright.
The Lord made Eden open, but man made barriers,
yet, the vast, briny ocean from all sin is free,
the tide rises and green swells break,
evil men like burning sand will surely bleed,
unbridled passions flow for the devil's sake.
Such love often lays rotten like man's greed
then the soothing tide returns to ease man's ache.

Summer

Come into my vision, waves of greenish foam!
Allow my bare feet to know your briny poem;
let the sea's tide coddle my lover's prayer and
form sonorous dreams that can ensnare!
Below the mountains so high and green,
the ocean shines so blue and clean as
the high waves approach my sandy scene.
The sun clothes my body in soft rays and
my thoughts travel back to youthful days.

The Sea's Current

As the ocean's current of green and blue
Rushes to the beach in foamy luminescence
Sages scrutinize the errors of careless time
Being washed brusquely upon the stony shore

Rivulets of briny white foam and brown kelp
Lie motionless, like forgotten memories
Atop the scorching yellow sand like the
Gnarled limbs of wooden warriors

Broken bits of long mislaid passions
Cry out so loudly; minds once incomprehensible
Amend mistaken preconceptions and observe
The immediate beauty surrounding their being

Quickly the unpredictable current retreats and
The beautiful mislaid remembrances disappear
Into the ebony depths of misplaced sobs and
The sea's current surges to a raucous roar

If only sages could stay the incoming current
Then thoughts buried in the deep would appear
Lost reminiscences could then quietly unfold and
Joyful meanings would be assured forever

Unhappiness would recede for a time and
The sea's fickle current would paint images
Of serenity upon the shell-laden shore and
All hearts would be filled with love

Driftwood Rhymes Upon the Beach

Tide tossed memories from my mind,
gnarled and misshapen like driftwood,
lie strewn cautiously upon shifting time;
Saline bits of warm recollections
washed ashore on salty dreams,
downy bits of knotty reminiscences
recreating long lost feelings of
yesterday's warm and youthful times:
Misshapen but undistorted in meaning, they
once again form beautiful oaken metaphors
for me to study and cherish in song and verse,
lovely smooth, tangled wooden poems written
lovingly in the soft, warm summer sand,
leading to future happy memories,
which will be tide-tossed upon my mind, and
will, once again, be remembered.

Briny Recollections

Standing next to misty hopes
while listening to the whispering
of the ocean's cheerless voice lingering
in the haze of a sad tomorrow's morn,
I become lost in the shadows of
past images of the rape of the ocean!
As I eavesdrop on the scarlet wounds of
the sea, my hollow eyes gaze at the stars,
which encounter the dark firmament with
unbridled anticipation! The melody of the tide
creates a nostalgia in my mind, salty notes
penetrate my senses with tears. How can
I stifle the melancholy I have of the horror,
what can I do to unlatch sentimental
thunder, which echoes in my aging mind?

The Mighty Power

The mighty power of the ever-rising sea
Drives the incoming waves of green and blue
Unto the beaconing sand, so white and warm:
Sea gulls and terns frantically twist and turn
In the shower of the water, picking morsels
From the brown seaweed that washes ashore.

The mighty power that thrusts the water onto the sand
Is the same power that drives the blood through every
Quivering body, the same power that drives the
Rushing steams through low valleys that were
Carved by the mighty power: The same mighty power
That gives sustenance to a mother's nurturing milk.

The child whose tiny hand stirs emotion in a
Mother's breast and turns men's fury
To quicksand is the power of birth and death:
The power that runs through the veins of all
Men and causes wars and chaos, as well as
The tempest storm and deadly calms.

The fallen blood of the mighty power fills the
Ocean with tombs of those who would be but
Never were. The mighty power of life and
Death, nourish the seeds of grand deeds and
The malevolent actions of despots, it lifts spirits
Of Saints, drowns the sorrow of the meek.

In the finality of the power, the tomb beacons,
The power dies, but the worm of death cannot
Stop the beginning of another mighty power.

It grows, in the nurturing womb of another woman
Who cultivates the mighty power in love, and
The mighty power rises once again.

Incoming Tide

Crusted colored gems sparkling
in the soft, green-stained sand
kiss the rushing, incoming tide;
translucent glowing colors hug
the receding sun, dipping into impossibilities.
Sirens entice me into the black velvet sea
and the obscure, graceless currents
pull me into deep coral portals,
where eel eyes of colorless blue
glare at the multiple facets
of my vanity and foolhardiness.

The Ocean's Silver Hue

The ocean's silver painted hue
reflects images from moon beams, which
echo the sadness of my thoughts.
As I muse alone, I long for a sorrowless song,
I search among the billion liquid lights
in the ebony velvetiness for answers;
I follow nightmares into the shadows
beyond the safety of my soul; and
where the colored jeweled-sea once gleamed,
I find only dull pebbles of sadness.
Only amid past memories of happiness
where my heart controls my brain,
only where there is no darkness, do
I find hope for the future.

Summer Time Has Gone

Thoughts of a gentle summer give flight as
Rains descend and rinse away the dust and
Then ascend to golden mountains of midsummer
While I listen to a distant cooler drummer:
Marching like an urchin that will transcend
The darker seasons and those they offend.

Colorful woven beads of a distant dream
Merge with vestiges of a glimmering time,
Leaving golden thoughts of a summer scheme
Lying next to a blazing fire and scents of thyme,
Easy conversations, hot tea and scented steam,
A brisk song spews from the kettle's chime.

Colder winds arrive but do not dismay
In the morn of this autumn day, then the
Holiday season brings things so gay, and
Thanksgiving and Christmas, not far away,
Encumber our nostalgic thoughts so true, and
The cold winter days seem not so blue.

Thoughts of Summer

Thoughts of summer have gone away
Now fading and no longer still:
The rains of fall have come to stay.

Gloomy vestiges of black and gray
Breezes arriving cold and still:
Thoughts of summer have gone away.

Warm views have left today
Flowing away into a tiny rill:
The rains of fall have come to stay.

The brilliant sun now has no sway
Autumn comes in quite shrill:
Thoughts of summer have gone away.

Warm beams from sun's ray
Now only a faded thrill:
The rains of fall have come to stay.

Balmy memories cannot stay
In the two story house upon a hill:
Thoughts of summer have gone away,
The rains of fall have come to stay.

My Son the Surfer

The surfer, board in hand, watches
as huge waves rush greedily
onto the sandy shore,
the man in black, with muscles
sinewy and strong, punches
through the body of the surf:
in his mind a picture, in his
voice a song,
he tips his board
toward earth's gritty chest, as
he dances to the rhythm
of the tide, his board skims
atop white foam, as the tumultuous
ocean holds him in the palm
of its salty hand,
he sways back and forth on
the opalescent crest, and
rides the mighty wave
to the welcoming sand.

Winter is Here

Sweet visions of warm sands are fading away,
The ocean's tide no longer calm and still:
The icy breath of winter is reflected in the snow.

Frozen streams and barren trees dismay,
My summer heart is abandoned and shrill:
Sweet visions of warm sands are fading away.

Cold thoughts linger as sunny dreams decay,
The mountains are white with winter's chill:
The icy breath of winter is reflected in the snow.

The unfriendly winds blow icy and gray,
Turning the sun to the iceman's will:
Sweet visions of warm sands are fading away.

Unfriendly gusts of winter are due again today,
Blowing warm thoughts far away from my hill:
The icy breath of winter is reflected in the snow.

In the months ahead, the cold wind will go away
Sunnier days will reflect upon a rill, but for now:
Sweet visions of warm sands are fading away, and
The icy breath of winter is reflected in the snow.

Tis Winter

Tis winter and downy birds
no longer sing,
bullfrogs on sides
of silent ponds only
croak in muted tones,
the lack of strident sounds
echo in the icy dell
so absolutely that
the hooded python
sleeps silently
in its black
winter cloak.

I miss the summer sun, and
gentle fall breezes,
the deep, clear ponds in which
we swam with
such abandon, I miss the
verdant valleys, the
narrow deer trails where
we walked for ever, and the
sandy beaches where we
conversed so happily.

In Winter's Icy Garden

In winter's icy garden,
love will not grow
amid barren roses and
dead pansies, low
in the icy times
of our disaffection;
amid the bitter dreams
of imperfection,
love starts to die
in the cold earth below.

In the freezing sky, stars
no longer glow, and
dreams of love disappear
as melting snow,
candied memoirs
no longer, sweet confection,
in winter's icy garden.

Your scarlet kisses
no longer flow: sweet
caresses no longer
for me to know,
your frigid touches and
words of defection, emit
dark rays of impending
disconnection,
a true omen of all the
things that sadly go,
in winter's
icy
garden.

The Coming of Winter

That time of year when warms days leave,
When the clouds amass and rains appear,
These are the times my heart doth grieve,
For cold days are damp, dark, and austere.
Without the rains, however, the earth would die
Flowers and trees would wilt away,
Without the snow children would cry,
A white Christmas would never be gay:
The rains bring spring, and a verdant scene
Colorful new flowers appear and trees have growth,
Without winter, nothing would ever be green.
I must admit, these gifts of winter I do not loathe
Without winter rains, there couldn't be both,
No new greenery or even gaudy birds.

January Days

Brisk cold winds blowing
Through barren birch trees,
Chanting wintry tunes through my mind,
They beget a cold apprehension

Sandstone boulders emerging
From a cold, tumultuous pool
Forming poignant doubts in my dreams;
Detached and distant thoughts emerge

Echoes of the winter wind
Rippling through whispered silence,
Stirring uneasiness in my body
And a sad melancholy in my mind

Cold, lingering murmurings
Echoing down steep, rocky trails
Carried by intense gusty winds,
Pierce the serenity of my existence

Mammoth pieces of dark granite
Reaching toward ghostly skies,
Painting shadows in my mind;
Restlessness fills my being

I long for the golden sun
And the rays of balmy zephyrs,
The melody of soft moving streams
And smooth warm afternoons.

Spring Arrives

The scarlet sunset passes gently through
wood-paned windows. Grayish pink shadows
glance off white, and gray-barked Birch trees
reflecting the vibrant whisper of spring's evening.
New growth sprouts from the damp earth. Herbs and
roses bounding with new life fill the garden,
newness is everywhere. As the sun escapes to the
horizon,
the gaudy songs of birds echo through the valley.
Large, vibrant clouds, pink with the remnant
of the escaping sun, just above the distant mountains,
shimmer heavenly as the twilight visits.

The Spring Garden

The sharp smell of new mown grass,
nature's beauty from a window's view,
bulbs leaving early in masse,
aromatic herbs growing out of a shoe,
tiny Pine Sisles flitting about,
old Australian dog sleeping in the sun,
a large mottled toad croaking with doubt,
an old striped Tomcat having its fun.
Gray ring-necked doves cooing in the yard,
sounding like the calling of an ancient bard,
singing quietly in his old raspy voice,
happy with the sounds of his rhythmic choice.

One Spring Evening

Serene was the evening without city roar,
A night of peace without scarred asphalt:
The wind's calm obeyed the earth's spin
As it kissed the sides of the smooth shore,
The sea's skin smooth as new blown glass
With gaudy birds strutting in its sand:
The stars, fixed with starlight gaze,
Shone upon a steadfast two as
They sat among the precious silence,
And stared at the glimmering moon above:
With her speech low, she wooed the night,
He held her tightly in love's gentle caress.

A Summer's Love

After winter departed,
after spring winds abated,
after cold breezes were gone, and
gray clouds had loosened
their sorrowful woes
in the verdant mountain streams,
which, hastened to rid
the moisture
of nature's deluge,
like old men release the
cares of aging;

Spring seeds carelessly
strewn upon the dell
by gaudy birds,
near summer's entrance,
blossomed, and
perfumed the verdant valley with
the aroma, of sweetness:

Billowing clouds of white and gray
swirled and scudded anxiously
atop fertile mountains,
craggy and steep,
young lovers' hearts
chimed in unison with nature's
blossoming newness.

Images of paintings of love and
white pirate ships, floating
amid towering castles,
gliding beneath
the warming sun,
impassioned young lovers'
hearts:

Amid the green moss, they
frolicked atop mossy ferns,
following the way
of all young lovers:

In summer's golden colors,
they became alive with
passions of youthful gaiety,
amorous in
Eve's garden of
delight.

To Be With You

To be with you on this summer day,
Most pleasant of all days,
Listening to leaves that softly murmur
And strident songs of gaudy birds
While the sunlight caresses your face,
The gentle breeze combs your hair.

To be alone with only you and
Observe butter-yellow butterflies flit
Under giant white-barked Sycamore trees,
Where only the breeze can be heard,
And filled with exciting delight,
Kiss your beckoning scarlet lips.

To hold you closely during pleasant hours
Under a beautiful sunny day's golden glow,
Listening to your dreams and wishes,
Telling you that I do not have to depart,
Then unafraid I quickly grasp your hand,
Ask you to never go away.

Then not hearing the din of humanity,
Only the beat of your heart,
I will hold you forever as the sea holds
The green current in its briny hands,
The heated sand grasps brown kelp,
I will embrace you forever in my dreams.

In the Caverns of Thy Mind

Within the deep, warm caverns of thy mind
Live lively thoughts and dreams that glow:
Like the sea's warm currents that softly flow,
They bequeath me soft memories of love divine,
Instill in thy mind the lost virtue of time.
Bitterness tries to cover these thoughts like snow,
It spews its spite upon thy life's theatrical show.
Then an inward truth clears thy mind in time,
It spurns not the beauty that lies deep within.
Let the voice of contented love speak today,
Allow it not to get lost within the cobalt sky.
Let it not become a fallow seed begetting sin,
Permit my feelings to grow and play,
Allow them not to decay into a lonely sigh.

A Lost Tale

I walked beside the moon on silver mist
And gazed at the starry heavens above
I was blown by the winds to where winds end
And reluctantly had to return again

I swam in the heated streams of delight
And journeyed on soft, loving rays of dreams
I laid on the soft warm sand and wondered
If the coyote really gave birth to the sun

I followed my fantasy in the still of the day
When the mountains were speckled with gold
It brought warmth to the strings of my heart
And played an enchanting aria of past times

And even if I don't remember the fable
Made up of silver smiles and cherry laughter
I know that someday some poet will write
About the beautiful tale, and I will remember.

When Time Departs

Scarlet roses surrounded by blossoming Thyme,
Stretching to welcome the bright morning sun,
The meandering Mint ends its daily quest of time,
Life's long journey ends and then I am done.

When years of my youth are finally through, and
The abundant gardens are no more, the sweet
Aroma will rise from a grave so black, so true, and
The abundant sky will open its vast indigo door.

Leaving

Leaving painful thoughts,
leaving hours of darkness,
leaving them,
unloosening my
lover's hand,
leaving our memories,
dreads, and fears
in the beat of my heart;

Leaving the lonely song,
death's lonely song,
death's dark, lonely song,
subtle and sorrowful
yet strident the notes,
to and fro they go,
filling the hours
of darkness,
waning and falling,
yet in the Fullness of the
orange and pink morning,
the sun replete with joy,
covers the gaping hole,
the darkness of the earth:

I leave her and leave
my song with her then,
gazing to the west with
silver beads upon my cheeks,
I communicate with her fleeting soul.

Adieu My Love

Quivering word unspoken
Lingering hand un-touching
Smoldering love dying silently

I am slowly parting
From the lonely shadows,
Stars flicker in overcast hearts

Roads faintly lighted
Endless unknown faces
Stirring in the afterglow

Melancholy footsteps
Pass silently by,
Embracing sad magic

In a doorway,
Memories of kisses sweet
Slowly ebbing away

Hurrying wheels
A boulevard harsh
Depot lights gleaming

Unfamiliar faces
Amid waiting crowds
Steel wheels shuffling

The iron path slithers
Into the afterglow,
City fades into stillness

The gasping engine
Hurdles into the night
Roads in vagueness mounting

Oh, amorphous illusion
Does her lovely soul
Understand my parting

My pale longings
Pasted upon cheerless
Lips of blue misery.

A New Song

The morning song, last remnants of a dark night,
Wondrous hymn of the wide-eyed starling,
The joyful ornate hymn, the echo in my soul,
The orange rising sun, its expression of hope,
With my lover clasping my hand nearing,
Nearing the edge of new memories of love,
In loving, we create a melodious hymn of joy,
A creation formed by the last remnants of a dark night.
When the dusk sinks into the gray horizon, and
A soaring excitement covers our bodies.

I Wanted to Tell You

I wanted to tell you amid the
vibrant tapestry with
the vivid colors, but
my rootless mind
became lost in the essence
of your beauty, in
the vibrations left by the colors
of your soul.

I wanted to tell you amid the
tight-laced weave
with its complex rhythm of
absurdities, but my
ears became lost in the honesty
of your voice,
in the reflections left by the truthfulness
of your being.

I wanted to tell you amid the sweet fragrance
of spices with the orange tang and
mahogany bittersweet bouquet, but
my senses became bewildered by the sweetness
of your scent, and your auburn hair's
sweet aroma that still lingers in my soul.

There is mystery to solving the enigma,
a complexity in the Calculus that
compels me to tell you
of my love, and it finds
me inadequate and alone in the essence
of your spirit, in the loneliness of gaudy rooms,
filled with intricately woven
carpets of love.

Love Danced

Love danced
in gaudy neon streets,
fiery dreams
hid in dark alleys,
where darkness
ruled,
dull moonlit beams
skimmed across
newly formed tears,
covering fears
clothed in yesterday:

Her hair
released aromas
of past loves,
of lilac scents, and
faded roses.

Scudding clouds
sheltered the fever
of passion,
bright lights reflected
the brevity of the
time offered
in Prometheus'
golden lair.

Bells
pealing in
a church's tower,
recognizing the
finality of the
ephemeral moment, and
youthful passion
chimed with a
garish pulse.

The Last Celebration

Sweet visions of the celebration are fading away,
The winter night is now cold and shrill:
The icy breath of my memory reflects in the snow.

Red wine and an empty chalice now dismay,
My broken heart is abandoned and still:
Sweet visions of the celebration are fading away.

Cold thoughts linger on as the wine turns gray,
My heart is frozen with the winter's chill:
The icy breath of my memory reflects in the snow.

That aroma of sweet wine no longer has a bouquet,
The dull moon is turning to the iceman's will:
Sweet visions of the celebration are fading away.

Unfriendly whispers of parting still replay,
Blowing cold thoughts into me like a poison pill:
The icy breath of my memory reflects in the snow.

In the year ahead, the cold wind will not stay, and
Sunnier days will arrive upon the hill: but for now
Sweet visions of the celebration are fading away,
The icy breath of my memory reflects in the snow.

In Memory of Claudia

The white saltbox sits proudly upon the hill,
The doors are open; it's very gay,
Memories of her are still aglow.

She has gone and it is very still
When the winds blow in the morning gray:
The white saltbox sits proudly upon the hill.

We look out our window with a thrill
We see her image as if it were today:
Memories of her are still aglow.

There is a memory that lies so still
It is as if she never went away:
The white saltbox sits proudly on the hill.

Her flower box is still placed upon a sill
Although the pretty flowers have gone astray:
Memories of her are still aglow.

Her long past thoughts still instill
Sweet aromas like a fresh bouquet:
The white saltbox sits proudly upon the hill,
Memories of her are still aglow.

Valentine Memories

He grasped the pink box tightly
With old, wrinkled, leathery hands
And gazed silently at the gentle decay
The morning crawled slowly across dew
The fair day quaked and swelled into blush

With a quickening, sudden surprise
The dark sachet opened to display
Hidden secrets that golden dreams
Had secreted away during blissful times
Youthful days and happier hours

A single glimpse revealed to him
A braid of auburn hair and a wrinkled
Note with fading, scribbled hand
Sentences of perfumed love adorned
Words of soft, endless promises

He suddenly withdrew inside himself
Hearing the lonely bells pealing
In muted roars, ringing in aging ears
He sighed in a mournful tone
Remembering her lovely smile

Leaning against his wooden cane
He dreamed tender thoughts
Of happy, bashful, youthful love
Drops of salty brine fell gently
Across deeply carved creases

He kindly closed his package of dreams
Looked across to withered bushes
In a dying flower garden filled with weeds
He lay down his tiring head and
Cried his sorrowful song of loss

The ruins of winter's rains had begun
The hours dividing, day and night briefer
Pale fruitless limbs and flowerless bushes
Withered vines once holding purple grapes
Gusty winds hurled adrift his thoughts

Warm summer morns and laughter gone
In its place only the obscurity of lost joy
Long shadows of dimming dreams
Hover over the vast cold, blue ocean
He dreams of vanishing vistas of sand

Tiny pebbles between his toes but
Hear only the wind speaking
In shadowy songs of yesterday
The melody of warmth is gone
This may be his last winter

He longs for hot sunny days
With which to thaw the coldness
Of icy winter thoughts of her death
Only a distant, forlorn emptiness
Lingers tightly in his aging mind.

My Sad Awakening

My feet press harshly upon the burning sand
With eyes half-open, confused images appear
Words arise then crumble as the sand shifts
Then warps into metaphors under my feet

The rough, pebbly parchment unfurls and
An ancient message written in sun-bleached ink
Deceives my sad and anxious memory
And causes my words to metathesize

Seeking to decipher the diseased meaning
Remembrances slip into the dark chill of my
Nightmares and a coldness not of
Winter enters into my dark sea-mist dreams

I creep into the melancholy of iciness
And the summer warmth slowly disappears
The hot sand transforms into snow as my
Mind struggles to regain lost purposes

An inner wintry storm disrupts my thoughts
My sacred intentions become opaque
And quickly metamorphize into ambiguities
The sanity of my mind becomes obscured

The enigmatically sad harmonics of
Cello strings vibrate in my pulsing heart
Subduing the prose within my forlorn
Soul as they deepen life's absurdities

The dark prism in my mind reflects
My contradictory beliefs and, like
A chameleon, suppresses the truth
Of all that I considered hallowed

Hidden within the darkness of my isms
A parable uncovers conflicting arguments
Within my being and carries my mind to the
Depths of inane anguish and absurdity

When I learned the truth of all that
I believed not to be true, I found
Myself unhappily in the company of
Angels, poets, and enlightened sages.

The Fern and the Spinet

In the corner of the room
where the northern sun doth peek so wearily,
She has her fern,
over forty years now,
crouching proudly by her aging Spinet:
Lace-like it is,
as if it had sucked the sweet cologne of Bach
into its aging leaves. I listened nightly
to the delicate bouquet of Beethoven
as it leapt from her fingers to my yearning ears,
the daintiness of her soft touch
caused my heart to burst, tears ran down my cheeks
as the soft tones touched my inner mind.

I felt so perfectly blessed
in the fragrance of her plaintive music that I
shuddered in fright
at the thought of her ever departing.

Then at night, and in my almost dream state,
I would strain to listen to her breathing
as I lay next to her in our bed. My heart
would leap with joy when the intake of her loving breath
did waft upon my face.

Speechless I would sigh and then
slumber in peace. Our elderly souls,
attuned to each other,
melt together like the notes of the Spinet's song
drifting softly upon my mind.

In my arms, she is so frail and sweet,
so small and delicate,
that I fear her loss.

Among the Spinet's sweet breathing, I linger
and watch my love as she caresses
the black and whites of life's song.
I sigh and try to remove my fear of her departing,
but I am aware as notes do fade away,
in time, she will, too,
and I weep within the deep and lonely
caverns of my mind.

I Feel the Fullness

The Kite Master
Let out more
String than he has;
It is now a lost memory.

Pine needles sinking deeper
Into patches of melting snow;
Sierra sunrise beaming down,
Orange upon pale white.

Dollhouse in the window – dolls broken,
One thread left holding an ivory arm,
Old frayed shoelace from
And old basketball shoe.

Warm rain before dawn,
Melting my iced memories,
Encircling a crimson nostalgia,
Seeping into my white noise.

Her images flow into me but
Unseen is a smile for me:
I feel a cold emptiness;
It surrounds my soul.

Gate to a Garden

The old wooden gate's moss hanging
Like a forgotten wedding dress,
Green oxide covering once
Splendid carved bronze hinges,
A dark mold stains the hasp.

How I envy your years, and
The thousands of hours
You opened to laughing children,
Youthful men and women, and
Serene octogenarians.

During special times of family, and
Gentle old age,
You were the gateway
To scented gardens of yellow,
Red, purple, and blue!

You were a secret place for
Beauty and ugliness, black and white,
All that was within, and without,
A bastion of serenity,
For all who entered!

You witnessed and participated
In life and death,
Happiness and sadness,
You remained an open portal
To the world, weary!

You were not just a garden entrance,
You were a safe, small
Refuge for dreamers
Large and small,
Young and old!

A Moonlit Eternity

I slipped onto a moonbeam,
which held my soul
forever in its
silver, sinewy hands,
my heart in its twisting pulsations,
my wandering spirit
in its infinite space;

It held me
in watery suspension
of trembling ripples, which
lifted me aloft to places
imaginary and beautiful, my
longing thoughts like
beautiful colored glass,
crashed upon
my searching mind and
coalesced
into yesterday's dreams
which, like a calm blue
today reflected upon
a moonlit
eternity.

The Moth's Madness

There is madness,
between truth and
duplicity;
a disconnect that I yearn to
reconnect.

I crave to be that which I can
not be, to know what is unknowable,
I decry the darkness of unreality, and
the deep ocean's mysteries,
which baffle the
philosopher's quest for
certainty.

I dream of an unreality which
screams to understand without
dilution,
a hunger that seeks things
imaginary.

As I immerse my feelings into
the silence of the caverns of
my searching mind, I spill my
broken memories into the
ambiguity of unexplained
truths, and without
any abstractions,
I listen to the sirens
howling in
my simmering mind.

Come to me so that I can listen
to your warmth and smell your
truthfulness, come to me so that
I can feel the sound of your voice and
smell the honesty of your winged essence.

Come with me to search the essence of
the truth of the tapered yellow flame;
let it consume us in its circling and
loving heat.

The Picture Album

Children grinning like happy ghosts,
Wide eyes, innocent smiles,
Discolored black and white pictures,
Parched and faded yellowed pages:
Names printed in faint, pale blue ink.

Images of clear lakes, rushing streams,
Blue oceans and sandy shores,
Verdant forests of vibrant green,
Birthday parties and camping trips,
Barbecues and birthday treats.

Pages of pictures of
Boisterous teenage years,
Basketball games,
Lowered Chevies, pretty girls,
Friends in white tees, Levi's.

Colored pictures emerge
Of a thin young man,
A beautiful new wife
Wearing a smile,
Holding a crutched man,

Pictures of college days,
Books, graduation rites,
A new desk, a new job,
A new house, new debt,
Then little children.

Newer images of children,
Clear lakes, rushing streams,
Blue oceans and sandy shores,
Verdant forests of vibrant green and
Memories begin anew.

Pictures of school years,
Books, graduation days,
A new desk, a new job,
A new house and new debt,
Then an empty nook....

New album, more pages, new pictures,
Children staring like happy ghosts,
Wide eyes, and innocent smiles,
Colorful pictures on white pages, with
Names written in bright blue ink.

Do Not Tell Me Lies

Do not tell me lies about
the green falling waves
that crash carelessly upon
the burning sand,
or massive rising
clouds which cling to the
bottom of the sky
in amazement;

Do not huddle in the back of
my dark earthbound brain, where
songs of yesterday still lie
silent and dormant:

Do not pull upon my
searching heart,
nor correct the rhymes
that echo noisily
inside my eager soul, or in the
unfulfilled longing
within my being.

Bring to me gaudy prisms
of beautiful, vibrant
colors that will reflect
delightful images
in my drifting senses;

Give me a desire,
a hunger for truth and
for all that
is delightful,
pleasing, and
alive!

A Simple Man's Prayer

Oh, Destiny! Let not thou be so sour:
I need thee desperately to escape this gloom,
In stagnant ocean waters so gray, so filled with doom.
In the midst of thy winter storm so dour,
Which I have forfeited to sadness in this final hour:
Oh, inward wretchedness, which arrived too soon
To even give my heart time to swoon or
Lift my soul to happiness high as a tower.
Allow our voices to soar again,
To bring a happy declaration to all thy earth:
My voice is too small alone against selfish men,
But yours is still pure and filled with worth:
Hear the muted prayers that dwell within,
Bring forth in our hearts warmth and mirth.

A New Morn

Remnants of dark winter nights fade away,
Orange arrives with the beginning of morn:
Memories of shadowy dreams no longer shrill.

The gloomy vestiges of darkness sway,
Warm thoughts in my soul are born:
Remnants of dark winter nights fade away.

New blissful thoughts arise today,
Darkness is driven away and torn:
Memories of shadowy dreams no longer shrill.

The warmth of the yellow rising sun will stay,
Past memories will no longer be forlorn:
Remnants of dark winter nights fade away.

I welcome the heat of the sun's loyal stay,
Into my heart its warmth flows untorn:
Memories of shadowy dreams no longer shrill.

Only ashen bits of darkness still dismay
In this happy place amid roses without a thorn:
Remnants of dark winter nights fade away,
Memories of shadowy dreams no longer shrill.

The Homeless Man

He is that stranger walking down the
Muddy roads of regret in small towns;
The wind blows the hollowness
Of his forgotten years into view.

His face is lined and haggard:
He staggers down a dusty path along the
Rusted iron tracks of an endless railroad
That leads to everywhere and nowhere.

Crawling out of his obscure mind,
He faces the darkening horizon
Of neverending mourning
And cries out in despair.

Murky, sorrowful scarlet memories
Of long-past battles of the lost war
Reflect off the rusted iron tracks:
Fading nightmares echo in his mind.

The hard dirt has been his bed,
A muddy stream his drink:
He sobs when the vanishing
Telephone poles twist in the cold.

His life has become a cavity,
A nightmare of unspeakable
Ennui and sorrowful regrets,
His tears are now dry and empty.

In the end, his only hope is exhaustion
And the cleansing of his weary mind:
With the serene blessings of sleep,
He creates illusionary dreams of hope.

In the cold, dank wind of a new morn,
He awakes to his daily nightmare
And begins again his lonely path to
That place, somewhere old and nowhere new.

Serenity

I recline upon my midnight dream and
Watch the stars soar in the sky,
The silence of the soft moonbeams
Soothe my aged and weary soul.

I balk at the philosopher's words
That tell me I must understand
The tenets of his murky creed
That befuddles my weary mind.

How can I appreciate the night?
Or the ending of another day,
By forgetting the beauty of stars,
Or the moon with a man's face
All made of green cheese.

I balk at the realist's words
That tell me I must clear my mind,
Moreover, never believe that fluffy clouds
Are made of marshmallows or pirate ships
That provide soft answers to my soul.

Wandering in My Dreams

I was drifting in my inner thoughts
Where earthly things ever disappear
And the fierce, opaque tide of my
Emotions crashed anxiously upon the
Shore of my lost and unexplored desires

My thinking was seized by translucent foam
And made a slave by the colored prisms
That refracted upon the facets of my soul
Salty tears washed ashore upon the
Youthful emotions in my doubtful mind

Ignorance came rushing in with the
Blue-foamed waves that crashed
Upon the granite rocks of obscurity
Imbedded in the dim caves of my being
And my thoughts became gloomy

I no longer discerned the contradictions
Harvested from the depths of the ocean
Which bled common sense from the
Ebbing, rushing tide of sane absurdity
The ocean waves of my inner thoughts

And the absurdities of my life
Liquefied into a dark yet new
Realization of life and mortality;
I discovered the inequities of life
And the reasons behind injustice

In a planet that had become brutal
I am now afraid to relate the
The truth for it would destroy
All remaining sanity in a torn
And severely battered world

Sad Times

Within the verdant pastures of my mind
scud the huge, white painted clouds of time.
Holding sweet thoughts of the past,
they flit in and out of imagination fast,
Like small wrens, searching for a safe strand,
youthful times of love and auburn hair, dainty hand;
Soft conversations, pretty, graceful smiles,
playful times sitting on warm sand,
watching white-foamed waves break upon the shore;
Why have the happy realities gone astray?
Did they leave with the years and left no more?
Why are we left with this sad today?
It whispers helplessly in our ears, and
leaves us only with a barren roar.

My Own Answers

I sit upon my midnight dream and
Watch the stars soar in the sky,
The silence of the soft moonbeams
Soothe my aged and weary soul.

I shrink at the philosopher's words
That tell me I must understand
The tenets of his murky creed,
That befuddles my weary mind.

I appreciate the early morn and
The ending of a starry night
By forgetting the reality of darkness
Or the full moon with a man's face
All made of green cheese.

I balk at the psychologist's words
That tell me I must clear my mind
To understand that fluffy clouds are
Not made of marshmallows or images
That tell me the answers to my soul.

I sit upon dark midnight dreams
Eschew the advice of experts
Scanning the heavens of my thoughts
To find my own answers to the
Anxiety I feel forever in my soul.

Somewhere in My Mind

Scarlet colors poking vividly through
The layers in the prism of my brain,
Blending with darkly painted ghostly dreams,
Reflecting and enlarging ambiguous questions
Of amorphous form, space, and matter, and
Mixing symbolic metaphors in dulled senses

Thoughts floating carelessly in the essence
Of the insatiable neverland of my existence
Are hurled to and fro by vaporous illusions
Primordial pseudo-ideas paint dark shadows
On fire-lit walls of my wandering mind,
Becoming mere ephemeral misperceptions

Images become darkened victims lost among
The blurred visions of my surreal world
And haunt daily deliberations of sanity
Sometimes I sit quietly in pockets of thoughts
While my mind perceives my emotions

Then in the mire of my experiencing
Uninvited crimson ethereal obsessions
The world implodes into blank nothingness
And I become contented in my insanity
Amidst all the other neurotic poets

My only illusion is that my dark existence
Will be stirred by some act of greed
And I will be forced to awaken to reality
And take pen again to express my outrage

The Past

I hear the pulse of the evening in my palm,
The murmurings of my memories strident: Shall I
Allow them to remain in the darkness, or
Strike a light and bring illumination?
The task may bring forth the truth, but
As the warm sand moves, and the kelp
Along the edge of the seashore uncovers the
Blackness of that which is below, I know
The truth will not always be easy to behold, and
I can lose the chimera of hasty decisions.
Can I stand to reveal the sins I left in the chamber
A long time ago while I was but a youth?

I grip reality, refuse the task of recollection, and
Feel the tranquility in my mind again;
It is not always wise to dwell upon the past.

Universality

Pain has no religion
Poverty has no nation
Disaster has no country

All colors of eyes have tears
All colors of skin feel pain
All colors of people feel sorrow

Every human has dreams
Every human has hopes
Every human has needs

All people hunger and thirst
All people dream and hope
All people yearn for love

Every creature is our brother
Every creature is our sister
Every creature needs others

We are all together
In this small, lonely
Place called earth

James Piatt | The Silent Pond

Previously Published Poetry Credits:

1. A Lost Tale (Front Porch Review)
2. Summer Time Has Gone (Magic Cat Press)
3. Tis Winter (Magic Cat Press)
4. The Oak Tree's Voices (Blue Pepper)
5. When Time Departs (Kritya: A Journal of Poetry)
6. Adieu (Kritya: A Journal of Poetry)
7. The Silent Pond (Kritya: A Journal of Poetry)
8. Love Danced
9. Leaving (Bumble Jacket Miscellany)
10. To Be With You
11. The Last Celebration (Kritya: A Journal of Poetry)
12. Summer (Long Story Short)
13. A Simple Man's Prayer (Tower Journal)
14. A New Morn (Long Story Short)
15. In the Caverns of Thy mind (Poetica Victorian)
16. The Homeless Man (Red Ochre Lit: A Journal)
17. A Soul at Peace (Penwood Review)
18. In the Meadow of Our Memories (Magic Cat Press)
19. Serenity (Taj Mahal Review)
20. Thoughts of Summer (Long Story Short)
21. Peaceful Silence of my Longings
22. An Ocean's Sonnet
23. The Sea's Current (Front Porch Review)
24. Beside a Brook (Magic Cat Press)
25. Coming of Spring
26. Wandering in my Dreams (Wilderness House Review)
27. Sad Times (Wilderness House Review)
28. The Coming of Winter (Wilderness House Review)
29. My Own Answers
30. Sunny Summer Days (Long Story Short)
31. Your Loving Presence (Kritya: A Journal of Poetry)
32. Driftwood Rhymes Upon the Beach (Westward Quarterly)
33. Images Reflected in a River (Front Porch Review)
34. Somewhere in my Mind (Pens on Fire)
35. In the Beauty of the Evening (Kritya: A Journal of Poetry)
36. The Past

37. Adieu My Love (VoxPoetica)
38. A New Song (Pens on Fire)
39. Briny Recollections (Magic Cat Press)
40. When Time Leaves (Magic Cat Press)
41. In Memory of Claudia
42. The Mighty Power
43. Valentine Memories (Word Catalyst Magazine)
44. Dreams (Kritya: A Journal of Poetry)
45. January Days (Word Catalyst Magazine)
46. My Sad Awakening (Wilderness House Review)
47. Winter is Here
48. A Lost Tale (Front Porch Review)
49. Incoming Tide (Illogical Muse)
50. The Fern and the Spinet (Bumble Jacket Miscellany)
51. I feel The Fullness (Counter Example: Poetics)
52. Gate to a Garden (WestWard Quarterly)
53. The Brook (Tower Journal)
54. One Spring Evening (Vox Poetica)
55. Mountain Top Experience (Greensilk Journal)
56. Spring Arrives (Phati'tude Literary journal)
57. Leaving (Bumble Jacket Miscellany)
58. Your Loving Presence (Kritya: A Journal of Poetry)
59. My Son the Surfer
60. In Winter's Icy Garden (Wilderness House Review)
61. Moonlit Eternity
62. The Moth's Madness
63. A Summer's Love
64. I Wanted to Tell You (Garbanzo Literary Journal)
65. After the Storm
66. The Spring Garden (Viral Cat)
67. Summer has Come to Stay
68. The Picture Album (Word Catalyst Magazine)
69. Do Not Tell Me Lies ((Bumble Jacket Miscellany)
70. Flowing (Bumble Jacket Miscellany)
71. One Spring Evening (Vox Poetica)
72. Atop a Mountain (Bumble Jacket Miscellany)
73. As I sit Alongside a Stream (Wilderness House Review)
74. Universality (Word Catalyst Magazine)

www.ingramcontent.com/pod-product-compliance
Lightning Source LLC
Chambersburg PA
CBHW071620040426
42452CB00009B/1419